Tell Me All
That You Know

The Unauthorized
Grateful Dead Trivia Book

BRIAN A. FOLKER

PINNACLE BOOKS

PINNACLE BOOKS are published by

Kensington Publishing Corp.
850 Third Avenue
New York, NY 10022

Pinnacle and the P logo Reg. U.S. Pat. & TM Off.

First Pinnacle Books Printing: May, 1996

Printed in the United States of America

10   9   8   7   6   5   4   3   2   1

"Tell me all that ya know . . ."

from Robert Hunter's "Birdsong"

Deadicated to those fans currently serving federal prison sentences for lifestyle crimes.

ACKNOWLEDGMENTS

First and foremost, a big thank you to those journalists who have watched and written about the Grateful Dead from the beginning while the mainstream media all but ignored one of pop culture's most complex phenomena. Their work was a valuable resource in the research of this book. Although they are too numerous to mention, particular thanks go to David Gans, Blair Jackson, Sandy Troy, Joel Selvin, Herb Greene, Jerilyn Brandelius, David Shenk, and Steve Silberman for jobs well done. Also, the staff at Relix for keeping us tuned in over the years.

Without my agent, Joe Ajlouny, this book couldn't have happened. Thanks to him for his work and encouragement across time zones. Also, thanks to Paul Dinas and Amy Garvey at Kensington Publishing.

A "house drink" to John Bloom for his tolerance and guidance.

Thanks to Tim Vall and friends, for letting us pick their brains.

The staff at the San Francisco Public Library and at the Oakland Public Library were of tremendous help. Sorry about the microfilm machine.

And, of course—to the Grateful Dead, and to all those involved with putting on the show. Thanks for making the trip.

CONTENTS

"Knock You Down, Beat You Up, and Give
Your Ass a Kick"

"Keep Your Day Job"

"We Played Terribly at Woodstock"

"The Sky Was Yellow and the Sun Was Blue"

"Honey, Come Quick with the Iodine"

"Arrows of Neon and Flashing Marquees Out
on Main Street"

FOREWORD

It was in some not quite midwestern town, maybe Pittsburgh or Cleveland, I can't remember which. After a particularly electrifying show, I was sitting in the parking lot on the hood of my car, clearing my head and praying there wasn't a police checkpoint between the front gate and the interstate.

My concern for the police was valid, for it was no time to run afoul of the law. The local gentry were feeling mean, and a heavy fog of doom blanketed the stadium. The media were questioning just why thousands of "transients" had descended on their fair city, buying granola bars and Gatorade and sleeping in the parking lots of 7-Elevens.

Carnival acts had been streaming into town for days, and even the airport had begun to resemble some warped medieval festival, with jingling bells and masses of jesters clad in tie-dye, suede, American flags, and Indian headresses. The odor of patchouli was so thick that airport security notified the local FBI office that there might have been some sort of chemical attack. A familiar sweet, sticky odor hung on the breeze and some people were exhibiting behavior that resembled the advanced stages of syphilis . . .

But while the papers were questioning why we were there, the authorities were wondering when we were leaving. Ironically, although they had braced for a wave of atrocities from this mob of long-haired freaks obviously out of their minds on God knew what, one group of fans cleaned up garbage at a city park and another volunteered at a local soup kitchen.

People were now pouring out of the stadium in a steady stream and bootleg tapes were already being played from car stereos, providing an instant flashback to the evening's performance. I was in the process of getting a blank tape out of the car to give to some stranger when a young man, buck naked, broke from the crowd, skipped across the parking lot, and disappeared into the night. No one noticed or looked twice.

I knew I was on to something good.

It's been almost thirty years since the Grateful Dead began their renegade rise to stardom. A lot has happened in those years. From their humble beginnings in Haight-Ashbury to the sellout stadium tours and music videos of today, the band has endured against amazing odds and still refuses to take itself too seriously. And so do I. When this project first came to mind, I wanted to create something fun to take on the road to pass the miles and engender lively discussion (and cause arguments) among friends. The questions contained within are of varying difficulty. The seasoned Deadhead may not be stumped by the majority of them, but I also wanted to give younger fans who just got on the bus a chance to test their knowledge and feed their heads with facts and anecdotes. My goal was to create a series of questions that were not too hard or too easy, and I think you'll find there is a little of both. If you really want a twist, try reading the answers and see what kind of questions you can come up with.

As this book was about to go to press, the Grateful Dead space shuttle crash-landed into reality. The old man had passed on, and for most of us the best chapter in life and the history of rock-and-roll ended on that August morning.

Jerry Garcia led a full life, was a fantastic musician and touched many lives. While the Grateful Dead trip as we know it has come to an end, we still have the music, the memories, and the many friends we made along the way.

Enjoy.

Brian Folker
San Francisco
November, 1995

"Goin' Where the Wind Don't Blow So Strange . . ."

Grateful Dead Geography

1. At what San Francisco address did the Grateful Dead reside during the mid 1960s, and which two band members did not live there?

2. Name the Palo Alto music store where Jerry Garcia and Ron "PigPen" McKernan first met.

3. From what country did Jerry Garcia's father emigrate?

4. Name the Menlo Park, California, pizza parlor where the Warlocks often played.

5. Where was the Trips Festival held?

6. From what country did rock promoter and Grateful Dead benefactor Bill Graham emigrate?

7. When and where was the Grateful Dead's first concert outside the United States?

8. When and where was the band's first European show?

9. In what U. S. city were three fans struck by lightning during the 1995 Summer Tour?

10. Which Grateful Dead album name is synonymous with a method of navigation used by sailors and pilots?

11. Where is "Lake Acid"?

12. Where is the Grateful Dead's studio, and what is it called?

13. Travelling through which European country inspired Robert Hunter to write "Ripple" and "To Lay Me Down"?

14. Why did Phil Lesh and Jerry Garcia switch places on stage in 1981?

ANSWERS

1. The band resided at 710 Ashbury Street, in San Francisco's Haight-Ashbury district. Phil Lesh and Bill Kreutzmann did not live there.

2. Swain's Music Store. PigPen got Jerry Garcia his first job there teaching guitar in 1962.

3. The elder Garcia, José, came to the United States from Spain in 1919 and played clarinet and saxophone in jazz bands. After being expelled from the musicians' union for working more shows than the union allowed, he bought a bar called the Four Hundred Club at First and Harrison Streets in San Francisco, which catered to the maritime community. He drowned in a fishing accident in 1952 and Jerry's mother Ruth ran the bar until it was sold to the state to make room for a freeway entrance.

4. Magoo's Pizza Parlor

5. Longshoreman's Memorial Hall on Fisherman's Wharf in San Francisco. The two-day party occurred on January 22 and 23, 1966.

6. Graham was born in Berlin and avoided the Holocaust by crossing Europe on foot. He eventually sailed to New York and was put in a foster home.

7. July 29, 1966, in Vancouver, British Columbia. It was also their first show outside California.

8. At Newcastle-under-Lyme, England, on May 24, 1970.

9. Washington, D.C. All three survived.

10. *Reckoning.* "Dead reckoning" involves determining the position of a plane or ship without the use of celestial reference points. Instead, position is determined by the record of course, distance covered, and estimated drift.

11. Lake Placid, New York, became "Lake Acid" when the Dead rolled through town. Fans took it upon themselves to remove or cover up the first two letters of "Placid" on various signs around town, including the one on the Hilton Hotel.

12. Club Front is located on Front Street in San Rafael, California.

13. England.

14. Lesh needed to be near Bill Kreutzmann's bass drum in order to keep time.

Vinyl and Venues

Grateful Dead Albums and Notable Shows

1. What album was the first live record ever made with a sixteen-track tape recorder?

2. When and where was PigPen's last show?

3. This popular phrase, penned by Bill Graham, was put on a billboard outside Winterland during the final show in the theater.

4. On the Grateful Dead's first album, what does the cryptic lettering at the top say?

5. What was the original name of what would become the second Fillmore West?

6. Who was "Blues for Allah" written for?

7. For what album did the band receive a Gold Record in 1972?

8. Who used to dress as Father Time during the New Year's shows?

9. In June of 1980 at a show in Portland, Oregon, the band played this appropriate song during the eruption of Mount St. Helen's.

10. Who shared the bill with the Grateful Dead

at the final Winterland show, and what movie was shown before the music started?

11. "New Speedway Boogie" was written in response to criticism over what event?

12. What are Tipper Gore's favorite Grateful Dead recordings?

13. At what venue was the "Touch of Grey" video recorded?

14. What was the first song Robert Hunter wrote in the physical presence of the Grateful Dead?

15. At the final show at the Fillmore East before it closed, what did the guests find pinned to each seat when they arrived?

16. What was the first album released on Grateful Dead Records?

17. On October 6, 1966, the Grateful Dead and Big Brother and the Holding Company played the Love Pageant Rally in Golden Gate Park. What event prompted the concert?

18. At the end of "Dark Star" on *What a Long, Strange Trip It's Been,* some unintelligible words are uttered. Whose voice speaks them?

19. Who was the song "Cassady" named after?

20. When did Winterland close?

21. Name the Egyptian venue where the band played in 1978.

22. What was placed at the top of the Great Pyramid during the second Egyptian show?

23. During the final Egyptian show on September 16, 1978, the band played during what rare cosmic event?

24. What were the Fillmore Fingers?

25. What type of insects made their debut on the album *Blues for Allah*?

26. What is the name of Bob Weir's dog, who is often credited on Grateful Dead albums and even made an appearance on *Reckoning*?

27. Which band members sang the national anthem at the San Francisco Giants home opener in 1993?

28. At what two venues was *Live/Dead* recorded?

29. During the "final run" at Winterland, before the band's 1974 hiatus, what phrase was printed on the tickets for the fifth and final night?

30. In what Grateful Dead album did the "Dead Freaks Unite!" message appear?

31. In the mid-1980s, "Tapers' Tickets" (tickets for concert areas reserved for audio taping) featured a portrait of this person known for his taping abilities.

32. On the back of the album *From the Mars Hotel* the words "ugly rumors" appear in upside down, backward lettering. What was the meaning behind the phrase?

33. On the album *Without a Net,* who played saxophone on "Eyes of the World"?

34. Who produced the Grateful Dead's first album?

35. On the band's first album and on *Live/Dead,* credits are given to one McGannahan Skjellyfetti. Why?

36. When and where did the traditional New Year's shows start?

37. What was the original name of the Fillmore East?

38. During this April Fool's show, the band opened with each musician on another's instrument. Where was this show, and who was on what instrument?

39. After the band's first album was released in March 1967, where was the release party held?

40. What Robert Hunter song was dropped from shows at the fans' request?

41. When was the next New Year's show scheduled?

42. The inhabitants of the Biosphere Two eco-pod in Arizona were hooked up to what Dead show via telephone link?

43. What was the title the band originally planned for their debut album?

44. Who did the Warlocks open for while playing a stint at the In Room in Belmont, California, in 1965?

45. What was the first Robert Hunter song the band recorded?

46. Who always played the "New Year's baby," complete with diaper, during the year-end shows?

47. How much were the tickets that caused fans to picket the band's first Winterland show on March 3, 1967?

48. The longest known version of "Dark Star," performed on May 11, 1972, at the Civic Hall in Rotterdam, Netherlands, was how long?

49. Who helped out on "U.S. Blues" at the Capitol Theater in Passaic, New Jersey, on March 30, 1980?

50. What does the Grateful Dead's road crew receive before every performance?

ANSWERS

1. *Live Dead*

2. The Hollywood Bowl, June 17, 1972. By this time Pigpen's health had deteriorated to the point that he couldn't sing.

3. "They're not the best at what they do, they're the only ones that do what they do."

4. "In the land of the dark, the ship of the sun is driven by the Grateful Dead."

5. The Carousel Ballroom

6. "Blues for Allah" was written in memory of King Faisal of Saudi Arabia, a fan of the Grateful Dead's who was assassinated in 1975.

7. *Live/Dead*

8. Bill Graham

9. *Fire on the Mountain*

10. New Riders of the Purple Sage and the Blues Brothers played. The movie *Animal House* was shown before the music started, and the Grateful Dead finished off the evening.

11. The stabbing death of a fan at the hands of Hell's Angels during a rock festival at Altamont

Speedway in 1970. Robert Hunter particularly aimed the song at rock critic Ralph J. Gleason, who claimed the promoters of the concert and the bands, including the Grateful Dead, Jefferson Airplane, and the Rolling Stones, were responsible for hiring the motorcycle club as security.

12. *Europe '72, Workingman's Dead,* and *American Beauty.* Gore also took her staff and son to a 1993 RFK show.

13. Laguna Seca Speedway in Monterey, California.

14. "Dark Star." Hunter was living in New Mexico and mailing the band his lyrics. Some of the earlier ones included "St. Stephen," "China Cat Sunflower," and "Alligator." The day Hunter arrived in San Francisco, weary from hitchhiking from New Mexico, he sat down with the band and wrote "Dark Star."

15. A red rose.

16. *Wake of the Flood.*

17. October 6, 1966, was the day LSD first became illegal in the United States. This event is also known as the Lunatic Protest Demonstration.

18. Robert Hunter's

19. The daughter of Eileen Law, a close friend of the band's. Some say the song was also written for Merry Prankster Neal Cassady.

20. New Year's Eve, 1978.

21. The Sound and Light Theater at the foot of the Great Pyramid. Slides of the concert were projected above the band during a show the following month at Winterland.

22. A Grateful Dead flag

23. A full lunar eclipse

24. The Fillmore Fingers were a basketball team made up of employees at the Fillmore West. The name came from Bill Graham's habit of flipping people off. They were known to play the Grateful Dead's road crew during intermissions in a competition called "The Toilet Bowl."

25. Crickets. A box of crickets was miked and recorded in slow, fast and backward mode and then the tracks were laid on the album. The crickets were later released on Bob Weir's ranch.

26. Otis. After his death a "Farewell to Otis" appeared in the liner notes of *In The Dark*.

27. Jerry Garcia, Vince Welnick and Bob Weir.

28. The Fillmore West and the Avalon Ballroom.

29. "The Last One"

30. The "Dead Freaks Unite!" message appeared in the *Skull & Roses* album. The last minute insert was the first attempt at organizing "Dead Freaks," which was a popular term until fans came to be known as "Deadheads." About 350 people responded to the message and the Grateful Dead offices soon had a mailing list of 25,000 people.

31. Tapers Tickets featured a portrait of Richard Nixon, the "King of Tapers."

32. "Ugly Rumors" was a humanitarian spoof on the phrase "Ugly Roomers" which referred to the transient residents of the Mars Hotel near the CBS studio in San Francisco where the band recorded their eleventh album. Although it was unusual for the band to be politically correct, their management rejected the more obvious "Ugly Roomers," believing that it would offend the hotel's residents. At one point the band considered shipping bars of soap (Mars Bars) with promotional copies of the album.

33. Jazz player Branford Marsalis. He also made several live appearances with the Grateful Dead in 1990.

34. David Hassinger

35. This name is used to credit songs where several people were involved in its composition. The name comes from Kenneth Patchen's book *Memoirs of a Sky Pornographer*.

36. December 31, 1966, at the Fillmore Auditorium. The Jefferson Airplane and Quicksilver Messenger Service also played that evening.

37. The Village Theater

38. Fans were surprised on April 1, 1980, at the Capitol Theater in Passaic, New Jersey when the show opened with Bob Weir on keyboards, Brent Mydland and Jerry Garcia on drums, Bill Kreutzmann on bass, Mickey Hart on rhythm guitar, and Phil Lesh on lead guitar.

39. Club Fugazi in San Francisco, California

40. "Day Job"

41. December 31, 1999

42. The 1991 New Year's show at the Oakland Coliseum

43. *No Left Turn Unstoned*

44. The Coasters

45. "Alligator"

46. Jim Haynie, a close friend of Bill Graham.

47. $3.50

48. 40 minutes

49. John Belushi

50. Steak and lobster

"Please Forget You Knew My Name . . ."

Grateful Dead Aliases

1. What were two nicknames Ron McKernan had before "PigPen"?

2. What were the Warlocks called before they went electric, and which members of the future Grateful Dead were in it?

3. In 1966 the Grateful Dead recorded six tracks for Autumn Records, including "Can't Come Down," "Mindbender," and "Caution—Don't Step on the Tracks." What name did the band go by?

4. Who was Bill Sommers, and what was his relationship to the band?

5. In 1989 authorities in Hampton, Virginia, refused to let the Grateful Dead play, so they went on under a different name. What was it?

6. Grateful Dead sound man and LSD chemist Owsley Stanley was known by another name. What is it, and how did he get his alias?

7. What is the nickname for the drummer's elaborate circular set of percussion instruments?

8. What were the "So-What Papers"?

9. PigPen's father was a famous Bay Area blues deejay. Name him.

10. What is Mountain Girl's real name?

11. What is Wavy Gravy's real name, and who gave him his alias?

12. Warner Brothers gave the band so much flak over the name of this album that they renamed it simply *Grateful Dead Live.*

13. What were two names the band considered before deciding on "the Grateful Dead"?

14. What was Bill Graham's real name, and what was the nickname the band gave him publicly that he hated so much?

15. On Robert Hunter's album *Tiger Rose,* a Grateful Dead drummer is credited as "B. D. Shot." Who is he, and what does "B. D. Shot" stand for?

16. Who was Anton Round?

17. What was the alternate title to *Europe '72*?

18. What was the working studio title to "U.S. Blues"?

19. What was the original title of *Aoxomoxoa*?

20. Who was Lefty Banks?

21. Which two band members do not go by their actual surnames?

22. Who was Clifton Hanger?

23. Who was Jerome John Garcia named after?

24. Who gave Jerry Garcia the nickname "Captain Trips"?

25. In what year did the Warlocks become the Grateful Dead?

26. What was another name once considered for the band?

27. According to Funk and Wagnalls, what is the meaning of "grateful dead"? Who discovered it as a name for the band?

28. What are the nicknames of three of the guitars Doug Irwin handcrafted for Jerry Garcia?

ANSWERS

1. PigPen was known as "Rims" and "Blue Ron."

2. Mother McCree's Uptown Jug Champions featured Jerry Garcia, PigPen, and Bob Weir.

3. The Emergency Crew

4. Bill Sommers was the name Bill Kreutzmann went by during the band's early days when they weren't old enough to play in bars. Bill Sommers was the name on his fake ID. When the band was busted for drugs in October of 1967, it was one Bill Sommers who was listed in the *San Francisco Chronicle* as one of the perpetrators.

5. They promoted the show as *Formerly the Warlocks*. This moniker was also used on January 14, 1966, for a San Francisco Mime Troupe Benefit at the Fillmore.

6. Owsley's nickname was "the Bear." He claims he was rather hairy as a child.

7. The Beast—introduced in 1979.

8. The *So-What Papers* were a ninety-three-page report by ex-Wall Street economist and Deadhead Ron Rakow discussing the feasibility

of the Grateful Dead forming their own record label. Subsequently, Grateful Dead Records became the first record company to be owned and operated by a rock band. When things went weird for the band in 1975, Rakow skimmed a large sum of cash and took off.

9. "Cool Breeze."

10. Carolyn Adams.

11. Wavy Gravy was known as Hugh Romney until he and his Hog Farm took on the task of feeding the masses at Woodstock. B. B. King officially gave him his nickname at the Texas International Pop Festival the following year. While performing as a stand-up comic, Wavy Gravy also went by the name "Al Dente."

12. The album was originally titled *Skullfuck*.

13. The band also considered the names "Vitamin E and the Vivisectionists," and "Here and Now and the Reality Sandwich."

14. Bill Graham's real name was Wolfgang Grajonca. The Grateful Dead did a show on his birthday one year and announced to the crowd that Graham's new name was "Uncle Bobo." Graham claimed that from then on he would hear "Hey, Uncle Bobo" whenever he was out in public. He

equated the name with "Uncle Shit" and pleaded with the band to give him a new name.

15. The drummer was Mickey Hart, who felt he had to sacrifice his style to perform on "Tiger Rose" and thus became "schizophrenic." "B. D. Shot" stands for bass drum, snare, high hat, overhead and tom-tom.

16. Anton Round was a nonexistent executive at Round Records whose signature was used (and blamed) for questionable business decisions such as shipping ceramic joint holders to radio stations along with promotional releases. Anton Round was the equivalent of signing your dog up for the Columbia House music club.

17. *Over There.* The band planned on reproducing a National Geographic magazine cover on the cover of the album but the magazine's lawyers canned the idea.

18. "U.S. Greys," also known in its early days as "Wave that Flag"

19. *Earthquake Country*

20. Lefty Banks was a stage name for Robert Hunter during his early solo performances.

21. Phil Lesh was born Philip Chapman, and Bob Weir was born Robert Hall.

22. Clifton Hanger was an alias that Brent Mydland used when checking into hotel rooms. When *Without a Net* was released shortly after Mydland's death, it was dedicated to Clifton Hanger.

23. Jerome Kern, a famous Broadway composer

24. The Merry Pranksters. It was a takeoff on Garcia's trademark Captain America hat.

25. 1965

26. The Mythical Ethical Icicle Tricycle

27. "Grateful dead" refers to a cyclical folk tale in which a man comes across a group of peasants mistreating a corpse. He pays for the burial. In a time of need, he had been befriended and helped by a stranger who turns out to be the man he buried. Jerry Garcia discovered the phrase while flipping through a dictionary.

28. Wolf, Tiger, and Rosebud

"Knock You Down, Beat You Up, and Give Your Ass a Kick . . ."

The Misadventures of the Grateful Dead

1. On the bus trip across Europe during the 1972 tour, there were two buses filled with the band, road crew, family, and friends. Since there were two buses there were two opposing factions. What were they called?

2. Warner Brothers staged a look-alike contest of this band member.

3. During the May 3, 1968, student strike at Columbia University, the campus was surrounded by police. How did the Grateful Dead get in to play?

4. Which band member was constantly mistaken for a girl?

5. In 1968, Jimi Hendrix set up a jam session with the Grateful Dead and then stood them up. How did they retaliate?

6. While the band was living in Marin County in the late 1960s, their neighbors were the Quicksilver Messenger Service. What childhood game did the two bands participate in?

7. In 1970 some "basement tapes" were released without the band's permission and put on the market by Sunflower and MGM. What were the two albums?

8. Why did Pacific Recording Studio sue the band in 1969?

9. This Washington, D.C., bureaucrat threatened to have the Grateful Dead banished from the nation's capital when he wasn't allowed backstage.

10. In the sixth grade, Bill Kreutzmann was thrown out of band class. Why?

11. The father of this band member briefly managed the band and was eventually sued for embezzlement.

12. Why was Jerry Garcia ejected from the U.S. Army?

13. In 1980, Radio City Music Hall and Rockefeller Center filed a $1.2 million suit in federal court against the Grateful Dead, claiming they defamed the theater. Why?

14. In his youthful days at 710 Ashbury, Bob Weir was known for launching these objects out the window at passing cars.

15. Before the June 14, 1985, show at the Greek Theater in Berkeley, California, the band's sound system blew during what Beatles song?

16. Why were the Grateful Dead driven from Lille, France, during the *Europe '72* tour?

17. Which airline banned the Grateful Dead?

18. Bill Graham earned a Bronze Star for saving a wounded soldier on the front lines in Korea, but for what other reason was his army career notable?

19. What city has requested compensation from the Grateful Dead to pay for the results of Deadheads residing there?

20. Who did Grateful Dead manager Rock Skully bunk with while serving four months in federal prison for a marijuana bust?

21. What happened to the original Warlocks bassist?

22. Why was Phil Lesh fired from the Post Office?

ANSWERS

1. The Bolos and the Bozos. The Bolo bus had seats that faced forward, and the Bozo bus had seats facing the rear. The Bozos wore masks and partied all night, while the Bolos slept. Whenever the buses stopped, the two groups would raid each other's provisions. They even went so far as to print a newsletter on their rivalry.

2. PigPen. Warner Brothers took out several full-page ads in *Rolling Stone* as a promotion for the *Aoxomoxoa* album, asking for a look-alike who could capture the "raunch" of "Mr. Pen." The first-place winner would walk away with $200 worth of Warner Brothers albums. (The pygmy from Venice Beach who wrote in and said "contests suck" didn't win.)

3. They were smuggled in in the back of a bread truck (Wonder Dead!).

4. Bob Weir.

5. The next night Hendrix showed up at the Avalon Ballroom, where the Grateful Dead were playing, and asked if he could join them onstage. The band said "Yes, after the next set." The set went on all night.

6. Cowboys and Indians. The bands would dress in appropriate attire and raid each other in the middle of the night. One night the Grateful Dead pulled a sneak attack and burst in dressed in Apache garb, complete with tomahawks and commenced to firing arrows into their walls. The night Quicksilver Messenger Service had planned their revenge, there was a riot in the Fillmore District and QSM, dressed in cowboy costumes, was arrested with their toy guns before they even got near the concert hall.

7. *Vintage Dead* and *Historic Dead.* The two albums were the result of bootleg recordings at Chet Helm's Avalon Ballroom at the corner of Van Ness and Sutter Streets in San Francisco. The Avalon served as a prime venue for music from 1966 through 1969, when it was shut down due to noise complaints.

8. The band had so much trouble with the studio they left their credit off the album *Aoxomoxoa.*

9. Congressman John Kasich

10. His teacher claimed he couldn't keep a beat.

11. Mickey Hart's father, Lenny Hart. The band estimated the elder Hart absconded with about

$150,000, of which $63,000 was eventually returned.

12. During his nine months as a soldier at San Francisco's historic Presidio, Garcia acquired two court-martials and eight AWOLs. He was finally characterized as "unfit for service" and discharged.

13. The suit stemmed from the Fifteenth Anniversary shows filmed at Radio City in 1980. The theater was disturbed by the "macabre skeletons" shown in promotional posters and references to illicit drugs shown in the video of the show. The suit was dropped when the band recalled the posters and removed references to drugs from the video.

14. Water balloons. Weir eventually gave up the prank when he was tossed in the clink for dousing one of San Francisco's finest.

15. "Sgt. Pepper's Lonely Hearts Club Band"

16. When the equipment truck didn't show, an angry mob, intent on seeing the Grateful Dead, forced the band to escape imminent danger by clamoring out a back window of the auditorium.

17. The Grateful Dead were no longer welcome in the friendly skies of United. As United management put it in a letter to Dead manager Rock

Skully: "Briefly, they have caused so much confusion arriving at the airport with all their equipment just a few minutes before flight departure, shouting obscenities at our employees and passengers, drawn and fired a revolver (fortunately, loaded only with blanks) at the check-in area . . ."

18. Three court martials

19. Santa Cruz, California. City officials claim fans shoplift from local businesses and fill up homeless shelters when they pass through town.

20. H. R. Haldeman, who was doing time for his role in the Watergate scandal. Skully claims he "learned a lot" from Haldeman but has refused to discuss even obscure details.

21. Dana Morgan, who returned from Vietnam with a drug problem, was replaced by Phil Lesh in the band. He disappeared and has not been heard from since 1983.

22. Someone on his route wrote in and said Lesh resembled "an unkempt monkey" on account of his hair.

"Keep Your Day Job . . ."

Grateful Dead Side Ventures

1. This short-lived bluegrass band featured Jerry Garcia, John Kahn, Peter Rowan, and David Grisman.

2. Name two of Mickey Hart's solo bands.

3. What was Bob Weir's high school band called?

4. While attending the University of California at Berkeley, Phil Lesh was the engineer on a folk music program on KPFA. What was its name?

5. In 1992 Bob Weir published a children's book. What was it called?

6. In 1972 several wives of the band members opened a boutique to occupy themselves while their husbands were working. What was its name?

7. Name two of Bob Weir's solo bands.

8. What was the name of the Grateful Dead booking agency?

9. When the Grateful Dead formed their own record company in 1973, they also created a label

that would accommodate their solo efforts. What was its name?

10. Why did a crow become the symbol of every album produced by the band under their own label?

11. What was the name of the band's travel agency?

12. What is the name of the company that publishes the Grateful Dead's songs, and where did the name come from?

13. What was Bob Weir's first solo album called?

14. What was Mickey Hart's first solo album called?

15. What was the name of the band's film production company?

16. What are the titles of Mickey Hart's books on percussion instruments?

17. While living in Haight-Ashbury, the band appeared as models in a clothing advertisement. What was the name of the store?

18. In the mid-1970s the band's road crew formed its own fly-by-night band. What was it called, and who was in it?

19. In 1963 Jerry Garcia was the star on Phil Lesh's hour-long radio program on KPFA. What was the name of the program?

20. What was Bill Kreutzmann's high school band called?

21. In 1968 a group of Grateful Dead associates, including veteran soundman Dan Healy, formed a company dedicated to wiping out the archaic sound systems they were forced to work with at the time. What was the name of the company?

22. Name the all-percussion band formed by Mickey Hart in 1975.

23. Bill Kreutzmann and his wife Shelley run what kind of business in California?

ANSWERS

1. Old and In the Way

2. The Hart Valley Drifters, and Mickey and the Hartbeats

3. The Uncalled Four

4. *The Midnight Special*

5. *Panther Dream*

6. Kumquat Mae. The store featured clothing, and, of course, Grateful Dead merchandise. Later they moved from San Anselmo to Mill Valley and renamed it Rainbow Arbor.

7. Bobby and the Midnights, and Bobby Ace and the Cards from the Bottom

8. Out of Town Tours

9. Round Records

10. Because there was so much controversy in the music world over whether the band could succeed on their own label that no matter what happened, "someone would have to eat that crow."

11. Fly-by-Night Travel. The agency also handled arrangements for New Riders of the Purple

Sage, Merle Saunders, and bands under the direction of Bill Graham.

12. Ice Nine Publishing. The name comes from Kurt Vonnegut's *Cat's Cradle.*

13. *Ace*

14. *Rolling Thunder*

15. Round Reels

16. *Planet of the Drums* and *Drumming at the Edge of Magic*

17. The Boutique Mnasidika

18. Sparky and the Ass Bites from Hell included Dan Healy, Rex Jackson, Steve Parish, Sparky, and Ramrod.

19. The Long Black Veil, named after a song that Garcia performed at the time

20. The Legends

21. Alembic

22. The Diga Rhythm Band.

23. The Lost Coast Kayak Adventures Company

"We Played Terribly at Woodstock . . ."

Three Days of Peace, Love, and Hell

1. What electrical problem plagued the band during their entire Woodstock performance?

2. At Woodstock, the band was loaded on LSD synthesized in what country?

3. Soon after it became clear that the festival was out of control, the organizers decided that each band needed to play a second set to keep the crowd content. The Grateful Dead and what other band refused to play without cash?

4. While negotiating the Grateful Dead's appearance at Woodstock, Bill Graham was adamant that this unknown musician also be allowed to play.

5. During the band's set at Woodstock, a stranger suddenly danced across the stage throwing what into the crowd?

6. How much were the Grateful Dead paid to play at Woodstock?

7. On the Woodstock soundtrack, what is Jerry

Garcia overheard saying during the segué into Arlo Guthrie's "Coming into Los Angeles"?

8. While the band was playing their set, what happened to the stage?

9. Why didn't the Grateful Dead appear in the movie *Woodstock?*

ANSWERS

1. Due to faulty wiring, they were shocked by their instruments. Random radio chatter also came out of their PA system.

2. Czechoslovakia

3. The Who

4. Carlos Santana

5. The infamous "brown acid"

6. According to a piece in *Variety* released after the festival, the Grateful Dead were paid a mere $2500. Jimi Hendrix topped the pay scale, cashing out at $18,000, while Blood, Sweat, and Tears came in second at $15,000.

7. "Marijuana—Exhibit A"

8. The ground turned to mud during the intense rains and the stage began sliding downhill.

9. Because their performance was "plumb atrocious," as Garcia often put it.

"The Sky Was Yellow and the Sun Was Blue . . ."

The Alleged Role of Illicit Substances in Grateful Dead History

1. During the Acid Tests the Grateful Dead collaborated with this eccentric comedy troupe led by one of the 1960s' hottest writers.

2. Of the original band members, who was the only one not into LSD?

3. Knowing that the band intended to "dose" him at some point, Bill Graham, in an effort to defend his lucidity, took to bringing his lunch to work in a bag, complete with a wax seal. How did he finally get "dosed"?

4. On October 2, 1967, the police raided 710 Ashbury Street and arrested eleven people for drugs, including Bob Weir and PigPen. What was found, and why were they released?

5. In 1977 the Grateful Dead were busted both on their way in and out of Canada for this innocent substance.

6. After the 1967 drug bust, the band held a press conference. On their table sat a cream pie. Why?

7. Who were the only band members not charged in the 1970 drug bust in New Orleans?

8. This addiction recovery support group named after a Grateful Dead song about a down-and-out transient offers support at concerts to keep recovering Deadheads off drugs.

9. What was the amount of bail required to release those band members arrested during the October 1967 drug bust?

10. Who was arrested *twice* over the raid at 710 Ashbury Street?

11. In January 1985, Jerry Garcia was arrested in Golden Gate Park while freebasing cocaine in his BMW. What caused police to approach Garcia's car?

12. What substance was listed as a production aid on the band's first album?

ANSWERS

1. Ken Kesey and the Merry Pranksters

2. PigPen

3. Knowing that Graham drank a lot of 7-Up, Mickey Hart put a drop of LSD on the lip of every can in the dressing room. Shortly after downing a can, Graham joined them onstage and played drums all night.

4. A pound of hashish and a pound of marijuana were found. Charges were eventually dropped because the cops had no search warrant.

5. Bee pollen, which was part of Bob Weir's diet at the time

6. The first reporter who asked a stupid question was to get the pie in the face; however, no one claimed the award. The Dead also served homemade cookies and cake along with coffee topped with whipped cream.

7. Tom Constenten and PigPen were not charged in the bust that occurred on January 30, 1970, at the same French Quarter hotel where the Jefferson Airplane had been arrested just weeks before. When the Grateful Dead returned to their

hotel after their show at the Warehouse, they found state and local police had already searched their rooms and were just waiting for them to return. The band was handcuffed together and herded outside the hotel for press photos. The incident was later mentioned in the song "Truckin'."

8. The Wharf Rats help fans trying to stay off drugs. Their meetings are similar to those of Alcoholics Anonymous but are tailored to Grateful Dead fans. Instead of reciting the Lord's Prayer at the end of a meeting, they recite the lyrics to "Black Peter". They can be located at shows by their trademark yellow balloons.

9. $500

10. Band manager Rock Skully was actually arrested twice over the raid at 710. After pleading not guilty to the original possession charges, Skully walked out of court only to be arrested again. Since the lease for 710 Ashbury was in his name, Skully was charged with "maintaining a house for the purpose of unlawfully selling, giving away, or using narcotics." He was released two hours later on $1,100 bail. He was eventually fined $200.

11. The car's registration was expired. Garcia was sentenced to a drug counseling program, and he also agreed to play a benefit show for the Haight-Ashbury Free Food Program.

12. Dexamyl ("speed").

"Honey, Come Quick with the Iodine . . ."

A Morbid Jaunt into Grateful Dead Annals

1. Which finger is Jerry Garcia missing, and what happened?

2. Who temporarily replaced Brent Mydland on keyboards after his death?

3. Name the town and cemetery where PigPen was laid to rest.

4. Mickey Hart suffered from this disorder in the 1960s.

5. What is the inscription on PigPen's tombstone?

6. In 1960 Jerry Garcia was in a bizarre car accident. What happened?

7. In 1986 Jerry Garcia fell into a coma brought on by what disease?

8. Public outcry and investigations into concert security followed the beating death of a young fan by security guards where?

9. What drug caused the death of Brent Mydland?

10. When PigPen's health began to fail, each band member contributed what to his recovery?

11. What is the name and location of the church where Jerry Garcia's funeral was held?

ANSWERS

1. He is missing his right middle finger. His brother Tiff accidentally chopped it off with a hatchet while cutting wood in the Santa Cruz mountains at age 4. A four-fingered handprint appears on the album cover collage of Garcia's first solo album.

2. Bruce Hornsby, who incidentally played in the 1970s in a Grateful Dead cover band called Bobby Hi-Test and the Octane Kids

3. The Alta Mesa Cemetery in Palo Alto, California

4. Insomnia

5. *PigPen was and is now forever one of the Grateful Dead*

6. The guitarist was thrown clear of the car and landed in a ditch; his shoes remained inside the car. Unfortunately, Garcia's friend Paul Speegle died in the crash. Garcia and Speegle had switched places in the car just before the accident.

7. Diabetes

8. Brendan Byrne Arena in East Rutherford, New Jersey

9. An overdose of morphine and cocaine—a "speedball." Puncture marks on Mydland's arm indicated that he was using drugs intravenously.

10. A pint of blood

11. St. Stephen's Episcopal church in Belvedere, California

"Arrows of Neon and Flashing Marquees Out on Main Street . . ."

Grateful Dead Film Ventures

1. Which band member codirected the film *So Far?*

2. *The Grateful Dead Movie* was filmed where?

3. Phil Lesh, Mickey Hart, and Bill Kreutzmann performed on the sound track for what feature film?

4. Jerry Garcia contributed to the theme song of the CBS remake of this 1960s television show.

5. This music video was so popular with its unique special effects that a video was made on the *making* of the video. What song?

6. Name four feature films Bill Graham appeared in.

7. In what film does actor Joe Pesci appear with a t-shirt advertising *Relix* magazine?

8. On November 11, 1978, Phil Lesh appeared on *Saturday Night Live* with a button on his shirt saying what?

9. In 1969 the Grateful Dead appeared on a television show sponsored by the publisher of this men's magazine.

10. After the release of the band's first album, they were asked to perform in a motion picture by Paramount. What was the film called, and who played the lead role?

11. Which band members appeared on the *Late Night with David Letterman* in April 1982, and what did they sing?

12. Jerry Garcia performed on the soundtrack of what movie prior to his death?

13. Filmmaker Oliver Stone asked the Grateful Dead to write and perform music for the closing credits of what film?

14. Which filmmaker created a feature film documentary of Deadheads called "Tie-Died"?

ANSWERS

1. Jerry Garcia

2. The movie was filmed during the fictional "final run" at Winterland in 1974 when the band planned on "retiring." The movie was released in 1977.

3. *Apocalypse Now.* The monstrous drum set "The Beast" was an extension of the drummers work on this film and became incorporated into the band's concerts.

4. *The Twilight Zone*

5. "Touch of Grey"

6. Graham had roles in *Apocalypse Now, The Cotton Club, Gardens of Stone,* and *Bugsy.*

7. *With Honors*

8. The button had the phrase "Hi Mom." Bob Weir also appeared on *SNL* in 1980 wearing bunny ears.

9. Hugh Hefner's *Playboy after Dark.*

10. The film was *The President's Analyst,* with James Coburn. The Grateful Dead were never in it.

11. Jerry Garcia and Bob Weir played "Deep Elem Blues" and "Monkey and the Engineer."

12. *Smoke*

13. *JFK.* Unfortunately, the band had to decline due to the project's short deadline.

14. Andrew Behar

Partners in Crime

Grateful Dead Collaborations

1. What husband-and-wife team joined the Grateful Dead in the early 1970s?

2. Who refers to the Grateful Dead as "the world's greatest garage band"?

3. Who was the band's first manager?

4. PigPen often went on drinking binges with this female rock star. Who was she, and what did they usually drink?

5. What protest singer performed with Jerry Garcia on the song "Clara Barton"?

6. What instrument did Jerry Garcia play in New Riders of the Purple Sage?

7. Who is the band's longtime sound man?

8. Keyboardist Vince Welnick played with what Bay Area band known for its elaborate stage shows?

9. This New Orleans jazz group frequently share the bill with the Grateful Dead.

10. These two individuals who aren't band mem-

bers play an active role in writing Grateful Dead songs.

11. Name two bands that Brent Mydland was in before joining the Grateful Dead in 1979.

12. The Merry Pranksters created an unusual instrument that is part drums, part horn, part harp, and part washtub base. The instrument is sometimes brought out at Grateful Dead concerts. What is it called, and who built it?

13. Jerry Garcia played pedal steel guitar on what Crosby, Stills, and Nash hit?

14. Name two Elvis Presley songs on which Donna Jean Godchaux sang backup.

15. On the Jefferson Airplane album *Surrealistic Pillow,* what position was Jerry Garcia credited with?

16. The Grateful Dead collaborated with this organization when counterfeit copies of *Wake of the Flood* began circulating in 1973.

17. Pig Pen was an honorary member of this notorious group.

ANSWERS

1. Keith and Donna Godchaux. Their last show with the Grateful Dead was in February 1979, at the Oakland Coliseum, for the Rock for Life Benefit. Keith was killed in a car accident in 1980.

2. Stephen Stills

3. Rock Skully

4. Pig Pen and Janis Joplin often drank Southern Comfort. PigPen was also fond of Ripple and Thunderbird.

5. Country Joe McDonald

6. Pedal steel guitar

7. Dan Healy

8. The Tubes

9. The Neville Brothers

10. Robert Hunter and John Barlow

11. Silver, and Batdorf & Rodney

12. The Thunder Machine was built by Ron Boise.

13. "Teach Your Children"

14. *Suspicious Minds* and *In the Ghetto.*

15. "musical and spiritual adviser"

16. The FBI

17. Hell's Angels

"If I Had The World To Give . . ."

Philanthropy and the Grateful Dead

1. In 1990 a group of musicians recorded a Grateful Dead tribute album. What was the album called, and what social cause did the proceeds go to?

2. The band worked with these two comedians for a Jerry Lewis telethon.

3. Who was the Rex Foundation named after?

4. The Grateful Dead provide funding to shunned composers from what part of the world?

5. The band is active in this charity group, founded by Wavy Gravy and the Hog Farm, which is wiping out blindness in third-world countries.

6. The Grateful Dead funded an Olympic basketball team from this country.

7. In October 1972 the band played a benefit show at Winterland for their road crew. Why?

8. Where do a portion of Cherry Garcia ice cream royalties go?

9. Which band member started the Further Foundation?

10. In 1992 the *New York Times* printed an op-ed piece written by Bob Weir. What was the subject?

ANSWERS

1. The album was called *Deadicated*. The profits went to the Rain Forest Action Network, which is active in stopping destruction of the world's rainforests.

2. Al Franken and Tom Davis

3. Rex Jackson, a road crew member who was killed in a car accident in 1976. This charity arm of the Grateful Dead hands out over $1 million a year to various environmental and social charities.

4. The United Kingdom. This was Phil Lesh's pet project to help out avant-garde composers.

5. SEVA, which means "service" in Sanskrit.

6. Lithuania

7. They needed capital to buy a house.

8. The Rex Foundation

9. Bob Weir started his own charitable organization, which focuses on the poor, the homeless, and particularly children.

10. Weir wrote an article critical of legislation that would open up the nation's forests for large-scale clear-cutting.

"The Medium Is the Message . . ."

Rock Art

1. Who designed the winged pyramid for the Grateful Dead's Egyptian shows?

2. What is artist Stanley Mouse's real name, and how did he get his nickname?

3. The skull-and-roses symbol is based on what ancient work of art?

4. The skeleton-and-roses design by Alton Kelly and Stanley Mouse first appeared on posters for what shows?

5. On the skull-and-lightning bolt symbol, how many teeth are in the skull and how many points are on the lightning bolt?

6. Who designed the dancing-bear icon?

7. Who designed the animation sequences in *The Grateful Dead Movie?*

8. Which Grateful Dead poster artist misspelled the band's name on a poster for a show at the Avalon Ballroom in 1966?

9. This "monster" appeared on early concert posters as a band member.

In the section below, match the album with the cover's artist.

10. *Shakedown Street* _____   A. Stanley Mouse

11. *Go to Heaven* _____   B. Bill Walker

12. *History of the Grateful Dead, Vol. 1* _____   C. Phil Garris

13. *Anthem of the Sun* _____   D. Gilbert Shelton

14. *Blues for Allah* _____   E. Bob Thomas

15. *Wake of the Flood* _____   F. Rick Griffin

ANSWERS

1. Alton Kelly

2. His real name is Stanley Miller. He got the name "Mouse" in high school because he was constantly drawing Mickey Mouse cartoons.

3. *The Rubaiyat of Omar Khayyam.*

4. Performances at the Avalon Ballroom.

5. The skull has eight teeth and the lightning bolt has thirteen points.

6. Jonathan Marks, a vendor of Grateful Dead paraphernalia. Marks wanted to capture the mood of every Deadhead at any time, thus the various jubilant states. The bears eventually made their way to official Grateful Dead recognition and began appearing on mail-order tickets in the 1980s.

7. Gary Gutierrez. The rumbling motorcycle sound was recorded live at Sears Point Raceway when Dan Healy miked a Harley Davidson chopper screaming up the drag.

8. Alton Kelly. He spelled it *Greatful Dead.*

9. Frankenstein

10. D, Gilbert Shelton

11. A, Stanley Mouse

12. E, Bob Thomas

13. B, Bill Walker

14. C, Phil Garris

15. F, Rick Griffin

"If Nothing Was Borrowed, Then Nothing Was Lent . . ."

The roots of some popular Grateful Dead songs

In addition to the Grateful Dead's repertoire of original songs, the band has performed and recorded tunes that have roots in a variety of musical styles spanning decades and even centuries. Borrowing from rock, folk, blues, gospel, jazz, and even disco, they have created a colorful portrait of frontier gamblers, assassins, cowboys, thieves, drunkards, lovers, sailors, and heroes. While some of the songs have appeared on the charts in altered incarnations, many have been passed down through generations in the farmhouses, freightyards, and shantytowns of the South and West.

"Dear Mr. Fantasy" was originally written and recorded by the British band Traffic.

Written and performed by Buddy Holly, "Not Fade Away" was also the Rolling Stones' first hit in the United States.

"All along the Watchtower" was a Bob Dylan tune as well as a Top 40 hit for Jimi Hendrix, who recorded it on *Electric Ladyland.*

Country-and-Western star Merle Haggard penned the outlaw prison tune "Mama Tried."

With its African-American origins, chant song "Iko-Iko" is popular around New Orleans and has been recorded by the Neville Brothers and Sugar Boy Crawford.

"Big Boss Man" was written by R&B artist Jimmy Reed, who had a hit with it in 1961.

Harry Belafonte made "Man Smart, Woman Smarter" a hit in 1965, although there is controversy about who actually wrote the song.

Skyrocketing up the charts in 1967, "I Second That Emotion" was originally a Smokey Robinson and the Miracles tune.

"Good Lovin'," written by Arthur Resnick and Rudy Clark, was a Young Rascals hit.

"Cold Rain and Snow" has its roots in the 1800s as a "white blues" song that came out of the Blue Ridge Mountain region. It was recorded by Obray Ramsey, but its author is unknown.

The Grateful Dead have been doing "Ain't It Crazy" since the days of Mother McCree's Up-town Jug Champions. It was written by the late

Sam "Lightnin' " Hopkins, a Texas blues singer.

Written by blues great Willie Dixon, "Little Red Rooster" with all of its sexual innuendo has also been recorded by the Doors and by the Rolling Stones.

A hit for Martha and the Vandellas in 1964, "Dancin' in the Streets" was recorded as a disco tune on *Terrapin Station.*

Country singer Marty Robbins shot to stardom after the 1959 release of "El Paso."

Jim Phillips of the Mamas and the Papas wrote "Me and My Uncle" but never recorded it. The song does, however, appear on a Judy Collins live album from the early 1960s.

First performed by Negro jug bands in the deep South, "New New Minglewood Blues" is about a textile factory in Tennessee. After each recording of the song, another word was added to the title.

A Donna Godchaux classic, "You Ain't Woman Enough" was first recorded by Loretta Lynn.

"Morning Dew," a chronicle of the cold war nuclear threat, was written by Canadian folk-singer Bonnie Dobson. The song has been recorded by many other artists in one form or another, and others have been given false credit for writing it.

Kris Kristofferson's songwriting debut, "Me and Bobby McGee," was a Roger Miller hit in 1969. Since then it has been recorded by Gordon Lightfoot, Janis Joplin, and Willie Nelson.

Many different forms of "Jackaroe" have been documented, some dating back to ancient Greek tales of a "maiden warrior" who dresses as a man to enlist in the navy to be with her lover.

"It Hurts Me Too" was written by the late Elmore James, one of the first blues artists to play electric slide guitar. The song was released in a posthumous collection of James's work.

Written by Eric Clapton during his Derek and the Dominoes days, "Keep on Growing" was released on that band's *Layla*.

A PigPen classic, "Hard to Handle" was written by Otis Redding and has since been recorded by the Black Crowes.

"Deep Elem Blues" dates back to the 1930s and recalls the Prohibition-era red-light district in downtown Dallas, Texas. It was first recorded by the Lone Star Cowboys in 1933.

Although it was first written and recorded by Chuck Berry, "Around and Around" was a hit for the Rolling Stones in 1964.

"Don't Ease Me In" was first performed by Ragtime Texas in the twenties, but it was also popular with folk and jug bands in the 1950s and 1960s.

"It's the Same Story the Crow Told Me . . ."

Grateful Dead Literature

1. Who wrote the first book on the Grateful Dead, and what was it called?

2. This host of *The Grateful Dead Hour* has written two books on the band. Who is he, and what are the names of the books?

3. Name three American magazines that exclusively cover the Grateful Dead.

4. The Grateful Dead appear in which of Tom Wolfe's books?

5. What two literary figures collaborated on the book *Garcia: A Signpost to New Space?*

6. In 1992 Tom Constanten published a memoir of the Bay Area music scene which covered his stint with the Grateful Dead. What was it called?

7. Herb Green wrote a book about the band titled what?

8. Jerilyn Brandelius is the author of what 1989 photo book that includes snapshots and personal reminiscences?

9. *One More Saturday Night,* which included an interview with "Mountain Girl," was written by Sandy Troy, who wrote what other Grateful Dead biography?

10. Blair Jackson, who wrote "Goin' Down the Road," also published what now-defunct Dead magazine?

11. What is the name of Europe's Grateful Dead magazine?

12. What is the significance of "Harrington Street," the title of Jerry Garcia's memoirs?

ANSWERS

1. *The Dead, Vol. 1* was written by Hank Harrison while the band was just beginning to attract a large fan base. Harrison managed the band for a brief time and has been accused of stretching the truth in his book. Incidentally, Harrison is the estranged father of Courtney Love, the lead singer of Hole and the widow of Kurt Cobain of Nirvana.

2. David Gans has written *Conversations with the Dead* and *Playing in the Band.*

3. *Relix, Dupree's Diamond News,* and *Unbroken Chain.*

4. *The Electric Kool-Aid Acid Test*

5. Jann Wenner, founder of *Rolling Stone,* and Charles Reich, author of *The Greening of America*

6. *Between Rock and Hard Places*

7. *Dead Days*

8. *The Grateful Dead Family Album*

9. *Captain Trips: A Biography of Jerry Garcia*

10. *The Golden Road*

11. *Spiral Light* is published by a group of Deadheads in England.

12. Harrington Street is a street in San Francisco where Garcia spent a large portion of his childhood in his grandparents' home. The book was completed by Deborah Koons Garcia and released posthumously.

"Please Don't Dominate the Rap, Jack"

Identify who said the selected phrase and what the subject was.

1. "I was a fuck-up . . . a juvenile delinquent . . . I failed school as a matter of defiance."

2. "While other kids were out playing cowboys and Indians, I was learning how to use a soldering iron."

3. "It scared me. They seemed to have—all that seemed to have—a connection to a very scary, possibly dangerous aspect of reality to me."

4. "Anybody who thinks I'm God should talk to my kids."

5. "Other investigations kept turning up the address 710 Ashbury as a supply source."

6. "It was just what I wanted, it was perfect."

7. "If the recording industry had its way, nothing would have a record button. If I had my way, *everything* would have a record button."

8. "I went down but refused to obey anything they told me."

9. "They are extremely transient and usually come to the area when there are shows in Oakland or San Francisco, and will at times stay between concert dates before moving on either to the next show, a Rainbow Gathering, or a similar counterculture event . . . For many, homelessness is literally a phase."

10. "We probably paid a lot of legal fees for people in jail."

11. "You've got the curse . . . they'll never leave."

12. "I was the only guy in a theater full of screaming chicks. I started to grow my hair long."

13. "The police and the legislatures and the business community—basically the people who were concerned with maintaining a stable society—saw this as a very threatening and frightening phenomenon."

14. "When someone knocks at the door, the toilet automatically flushes your stash."

ANSWERS

1. Jerry Garcia, on secondary education

2. Grateful Dead soundman Dan Healy, on his beginnings as an audio genius

3. Owsley Stanley, on the first time he saw the Grateful Dead play at Muir Beach

4. Jerry Garcia, on Deadheads thinking he's God

5. California State Narcotics chief Matthew O'Conner, discussing why 710 Ashbury was raided for drugs in the fall of 1967

6. Jerry Garcia, on his discovery of marijuana at age 15

7. Dan Healy's view of bootleg recordings of live shows

8. Bob Weir, on attending his induction physical for the military during the Vietnam War

9. The San Francisco Department of Public Health, on the homeless population of Haight-Ashbury

10. Bob Weir, on playing a regretful Black Panther benefit concert at the Oakland Auditorium on March 5, 1971

11. Jerry Garcia, referring to the influx of Deadheads invading the solo concerts of those performers who have played with the Grateful Dead

12. Phil Lesh, on seeing the Beatles' movie *It's a Hard Day's Night.*

13. Owsley Stanley, on the advent of LSD

14. Jay Leno, on the J. Garcia Suite at LA's Beverly Prescott Hotel. For $255–300 a night, guests get a room furnished with Garcia-designed fabrics and paintings.

"As the Storyteller Speaks . . ."

How Well Do You Know the Lyrics?

1. In the song "Wharf Rat," why does August West ask the narrator for a dime?
    a. For a glass of whiskey
    b. For a cup of coffee
    c. For a gin-fizz
    d. For a glass of grenadine

2. What happens wherever "St. Stephen" goes?
    a. It always rains
    b. The rent never gets paid
    c. The people all complain
    d. He ignores the pain

3. In "Cumberland Blues," what is the narrator's salary?
    a. $5 a day
    b. Two bits a day
    c. $10 a week
    d. A twenty-dollar bill

4. What does Satan take from our victim in "Friend of the Devil"?
    a. A twenty dollar bill
    b. A golden string fiddle
    c. His soul
    d. The strings of his heart

5. How much does the "Dire Wolf" weigh?
    a. 1000 pounds
    b. 500 pounds
    c. 600 pounds
    d. 800 pounds

6. Name the bar where "Stagger Lee" met his death.
    a. Dew Drop Inn
    b. The Lion's Club
    c. 2 A.M. Club
    d. DeLyon's Club

7. What color is Annie's hair in "It Must Have Been the Roses"?
    a. Blond
    b. Red
    c. Black
    d. Brown

8. What does one need to consume before "heading down to Minglewood"?
    a. A bottle of red whiskey
    b. Rye
    c. Couple shots of whiskey
    d. A jelly roll

9. On what day does "Jack Straw" leave Texas?
    a. St. Patrick's Day
    b. Christmas Eve

c. Fourth of July
d. Veterans Day

10. What city does Jack Straw call home?
    a. Kansas City
    b. New Orleans
    c. San Francisco
    d. Wichita

11. In what year did Esau kill the hunter?
    a. 1973
    b. 1922
    c. 1969
    d. 1953

12. What hangs at the top of "Franklin's Tower"?
    a. A guard post
    b. A bell
    c. A clock
    d. A guitar

13. In what year did Gentle Jack Jones step to the bar?
    a. 1920
    b. 1930
    c. 1950
    d. 1969

14. How many "teeth in a jawbone"?
    a. 64
    b. 18
    c. 32
    d. 21

15. What vehicle can "Sugar Magnolia" be compared to?
    a. A VW
    b. A Jeep Willy's
    c. A hearse
    d. A Cadillac

16. What famous mass murderer is mentioned in "Ramble on Rose"?
    a. The Boston Strangler
    b. Charles Manson
    c. Jack the Ripper
    d. Adolph Hitler

17. Who's been "way too long at sea"?
    a. Uncle Sam
    b. The Lost Sailor
    c. The ship of fools
    d. Row Jimmy

18. What might be found in a drain ditch?
    a. An alligator
    b. A passenger

    c. A cat
    d. A rat

19. Who is calling "Cosmic Charlie"?
    a. His wife
    b. His brother
    c. His momma
    d. His father

20. What time does Casey Jones leave Central Station?
    a. Seventeen to
    b. Quarter to nine
    c. Ten after three
    d. Half past nine

21. How often does one "need a miracle"?
    a. Once a week
    b. On the hour
    c. Every day
    d. All the time

22. How many "Tons of Steel" are out of control?
    a. 900,000
    b. 1,000
    c. 2,000
    d. 50

23. How long has our narrator been gambling in "Deal"?
   a. A month of Sundays
   b. Since he was an itch in his Daddy's pants
   c. Ten years
   d. All his life

24. Who was the "cool fool" and "never could do no wrong"?
   a. Annie
   b. Althea
   c. Sugaree
   d. Casey Jones

25. In what direction would you want to be a headlight on a train?
   a. Westbound
   b. Southbound
   c. Eastbound
   d. Northbound

26. What was the soldier's strength in "Lady with a Fan"?
   a. Strategy
   b. Honesty
   c. Loneliness
   d. Poise

27. In "Touch of Grey," what is the cow giving?
   a. Gasoline

b. Milk

c. Kerosene

d. Gin

28. Where is the party held in "One More Saturday Night"?

a. Town Hall

b. Courthouse

c. Armory

d. Church

29. What is the still fired with in "Brown-Eyed Women"?

a. Coal

b. Pine

c. Hickory

d. Redwood

30. How many days have "Me and My Uncle" been in the saddle?

a. One week

b. Two days

c. Three days

d. One month

31. In "Bertha," where does our protagonist take shelter during the rainstorm?

a. A bar

b. The jailhouse

c. A bordello
d. The sea

32. What town is "too close to New Orleans"?
    a. New York
    b. Tulsa
    c. Santa Fe
    d. Houston

33. What is the body temperature of "Black Peter"?
    a. 105
    b. 103
    c. 98.5
    d. 100

34. What is a wild card in "Doing that Rag"?
    a. Quecns
    b. Kings
    c. Aces
    d. Deuces

35. What well known disk jockey is mentioned in "Ramble on Rose"?
    a. Dick Clark
    b. Cool Breeze
    c. Wolfman Jack
    d. Don Imus

36. What type of tree is planted in "Brokedown Palace"?
    a. Pine
    b. Bonsai
    c. Willow
    d. Palm

37. In "Brown-Eyed Women," what is Jack Jones's wife's name?
    a. Sandy
    b. Delilah
    c. Bertha
    d. Mary

38. What line in the song "Built to Last" is also the name of a Beatles song?
    a. "A Day in the Life"
    b. "Got to Get You into My Life"
    c. "Here Comes the Sun"
    d. "I Wanna Hold Your Hand"

39. What article of clothing is mentioned in "China Cat Sunflower"?
    a. Scarf
    b. Sweater
    c. Kimono
    d. Waistcoat

40. What type of drink does Delia DeLyon ask Stagger Lee to buy her?

    a. A gin fizz
    b. A martini
    c. Mateus
    d. Burgundy

41. In "Dire Wolf," what does the narrator have for supper?
    a. Steak
    b. Lobster
    c. Red whiskey
    d. Beans

42. What famous painting is mentioned in "Foolish Heart"?
    a. Starry Starry Night
    b. Mona Lisa
    c. The White Girl
    d. The Lovers

43. How many different cards are mentioned in "Loser"?
    a. one
    b. two
    c. three
    d. four

44. In "Mississippi Half-Step Uptown Toodle-loo," what is the cue ball made of?
    a. Steel
    b. Styrofoam

    c. Cardboard

    d. Whipped cream

45. What type of weapon is the focal point of "Mister Charlie"?

    a. a knife

    b. a pistol

    c. a shotgun

    d. brass knuckles

46. What fictional monster appears in "Ramble on Rose"?

    a. The Hunchback

    b. Dracula

    c. Frankenstein

    d. Satan

47. What is the setting for "Scarlet Begonias"?

    a. Mallory Square

    b. Times Square

    c. Union Square

    d. Grosvenor Square

48. What is Uncle Sam's pulse in "U.S. Blues"?

    a. 72

    b. 105

    c. 87

    d. 91

49. What is August West's beverage of choice?

    a. Tequila

   b. Gin
   c. Burgundy
   d. Ale

50. What color is Moses's buckle?
   a. Black
   b. Silver
   c. Gold
   d. Gray

In each of the following questions, two words and a phrase are presented. Identify what Grateful Dead song they come from.

51. Despair . . . spiral . . . crickets and cicadas sing

52. Ear . . . rattlesnake . . . the latest mystery killer that you saw on channel four

53. Lightning . . . turning . . won't you try just a little bit harder?

54. Sunbells . . . mermaids . . . all Mohammed's men

55. Docks . . . crime . . . true to me, true to my dying day

56. Goat . . . wealth . . . summertime done come and gone

57. Danger . . . cannonballs . . . are you kind?

58. Neon . . . true love . . . got a tip they're gonna kick the door in again

59. Clover . . . dreaming . . . one last time

60. Highway sign . . . tracks . . . it'll do you fine

61. Diesel train . . . news report . . . you can see that it's true

62. Law . . . slot machine . . . Honey, come quick with the iodine

63. Silver dollar . . . alligator wine . . . gonna scare you up and shoot you

64. Abilene . . . coffee . . . last fair deal in the country, Sweet Suzy

65. Long shot . . . dollar . . . nine to five and a place to crash

66. Company . . . ribbons . . . faded is the crimson

67. Pistol . . . dogs . . . going where the wind don't blow so strange

68. Angel . . . crippled . . . without love, day to day, insanity's king

69. Critic . . . homeland . . . sometimes we live in no particular way but our own

70. Jewelry . . . trigger . . . jelly roll will drive you stone mad

71. Rainbow . . . carousel ride . . . gone are the days we stopped to decide

72. Gown . . . bandana . . . comic book colors on a violin river

73. Courthouse . . . Twenty-third Psalm . . . ain't no call to worry the jury

74. Tongue . . . dreams . . . when there were no strings to play you played to me

75. Running . . . jailhouse . . . I wonder if you care

76. Pillow . . . tears . . . when the moon splits the southwest horizon

77. Utah . . . levee . . . got a wife in Chino

78. Spurs . . . left-hand monkey wrench . . . I asked him for water, he poured me some wine

79. Pans . . . shoes . . . maybe try it two times, maybe more

80. Proposition . . . drifting . . . now I cannot share your laughter

81. Wagon . . . jubilee . . . had everything sewed up tight

82. Mob . . . highway . . . but I didn't have one good word to say

83. Yo-yo . . . fruit . . . shadow in the alley turned out all my lights

84. Abel . . . Rio Grande . . . farewell to you, old southern sky

85. Merchant . . . Tom Banjo . . . hey the white wheat waving in the wind

86. Jack . . . horse . . . in the heat of the sun a man died of cold

87. Daybreak . . . sin . . . world at my command

88. Mary Shelley . . . sailor . . . take you to the leader of the band

89. Harp . . . pebble . . . if you should stand, then who's to guide you?

90. Garland . . . treasons . . . darkness shrugs and bids the day goodbye

91. Barroom . . . dragon . . . the flame from your stage has now spread to the floor

92. Politicians . . . possibilities . . . it's all too clear we're on our own

93. Clowns . . . angels . . . bite the hand that breaks your bread

94. Heels . . . gentlemen . . . sweet as Spanish sherry wine

95. Wildflower . . . hounds . . . if you plant ice, you're gonna harvest wind

96. Goodbye . . . muddy . . . the line is busted, the last one I saw

97. Serenade . . . heaven . . . would you have the time to watch it shine?

98. Eagle . . . lizard . . . I say what I mean and I don't give a damn

99. Violet . . . cuckoo . . . she can wade in a drop of dew

100. Sleeping . . . moth . . . walk into splintered sunlight

101. Yoke . . . grenadine . . . tumbledown shack in Bigfoot County

ANSWERS

1. For a cup of coffee
2. "The people all complain"
3. Five dollars a day
4. A twenty dollar bill
5. 600 pounds
6. DeLyon's Club
7. Brown
8. "Couple shots of whiskey"
9. Fourth of July
10. Wichita
11. 1969
12. A bell
13. 1920
14. 32
15. A Jeep Willy's
16. Jack the Ripper
17. The Lost Sailor
18. A rat
19. His momma
20. Quarter to nine
21. Every day
22. 900,000
23. Ten years
24. Sugaree
25. Northbound
26. Strategy
27. Kerosene
28. Armory
29. Hickory wood
30. Three days
31. In a bar
32. Houston
33. 105
34. Deuces
35. Wolfman Jack
36. A willow
37. Delilah
38. "Here Comes the Sun"
39. A kimono
40. A gin fizz
41. Red whiskey
42. Mona Lisa
43. 2
44. Styrofoam
45. A shotgun

46. Frankenstein
47. Grosvenor Square
48. Seventy-two
49. Burgundy
50. Silver
51. "Terrapin Station"
52. "When Push Comes to Shove"
53. "The Wheel"
54. "What's Become of the Baby?"
55. "Wharf Rat"
56. "U. S. Blues"
57. "Uncle John's Band"
58. "Truckin' "
59. "To Lay Me Down"
60. "Till the Morning Comes"
61. "They Love Each Other"
62. "Tennessee Jed"
63. "Mister Charlie"
64. "Loser"
65. "Keep Your Day Job"
66. "Must Have Been the Roses"
67. "He's Gone"
68. "Help on the Way"
69. "Eyes of the World"
70. "Dupree's Diamond Blues"
71. "Crazy Fingers"
72. "China Cat Sunflower"
73. "Alabama Getaway"
74. "Attics of My Life"
75. "Bertha"
76. "Black Muddy River"
77. "Friend of the Devil"
78. "Greatest Story Ever Told"

"There's Nothing Left to Do but Count the Years . . ."

A Linear Look at the Band's Evolution

3/15/40—Phil Lesh born Phillip Chapman in Berkeley, California.

6/23/41—Robert Hunter born in Arroyo Grande, California

8/1/42—Jerry Garcia born in San Francisco, California

9/11/43—Mickey Hart born in Brooklyn, New York

9/8/45—Ron "PigPen" McKernan born in San Bruno, California

5/7/46—Bill Kreutzmann born in Palo Alto, California

10/16/47—Bob Weir born Robert Hall

7/19/48—Keith Godchaux born in Concord, California

2/2/51—Vince Welnick born

10/21/52—Brent Mydland born in West Germany

6/65—Phil Lesh joins the Warlocks

12/4/65—First show as the Grateful Dead

5/19/66—First show at the Avalon Ballroom

3/17/67—The band's debut album, *Grateful Dead,* is released

6/28/67—Monterey Pop Festival in Monterey, California

9/29/67—Mickey Hart joins the Grateful Dead and plays the Straight Theater

10/2/67—The Grateful Dead's residence at 710 Ashbury Street is raided and authorities arrest several band members and friends for possession of marijuana and hashish

7/18/68—The Dead's second album, *Anthem of the Sun,* is released

11/68—Tom Constanten joins the Grateful Dead on piano, organ, and harpsichord

6/20/69—*Aoxomoxoa* is released

11/10/69—*Live/Dead* is released

12/69—Hell's Angels stab a concert goer to death during a show featuring the Rolling Stones, Jefferson Airplane, and the Grateful Dead at Altamont Speedway

1/31/70—The band minus PigPen and Tom Constanten are arrested for drug posession in New Orleans; the charges are eventually dismissed.

1/70—Tom Constanten leaves the band

5/12/70—*Workingman's Dead* is released

11/70—The band's sixth album, *American Beauty,* is released

2/71—Mickey Hart leaves the Grateful Dead

10/71—*Skullfuck* is released.

10/19/71—Keith Godchaux joins the Grateful Dead

12/31/71—Donna Godchaux joins the band

6/17/72—PigPen plays his last show at the Hollywood Bowl

11/72—*Europe '72* is released

3/8/73—PigPen dies of a stomach hemorrhage brought on by alcoholism

7/13/73—*History of the Grateful Dead (Bear's Choice)* is released

11/73—*Wake of the Flood* is released on Grateful Dead Records

3/23/74—The Wall of Sound debuts at the Cow Palace in Daly City, California

6/74—*From the Mars Hotel* is released

10/74—The "Final Run" at Winterland; Mickey Hart rejoins the band

9/75—*Blues for Allah* released

4/76—Grateful Dead records begins to fold

6/76—*Steal Your Face* is released

6/77—*The Grateful Dead Movie* is released featuring footage of the final shows at Winterland in October 1974

7/77—*Terrapin Station* is released

11/78—*Shakedown Street* is released

2/79—Keith and Donna Godchaux leave the Grateful Dead

4/79—Brent Mydland joins the Grateful Dead

4/80—*Go to Heaven* is released

7/23/80—Keith Godchaux dies in a car accident in Marin County, California

4/1/81—*Reckoning* is released

8/81—*Dead Set* is released

1/18/85—Jerry Garcia is arrested in Golden Gate Park while freebasing cocaine in his car; he is ordered into a rehabilitation program and agrees to play a benefit concert for the Haight-Ashbury Free Food Program

7/10/86—Jerry Garcia falls into a diabetic coma and the future of the Grateful Dead hangs in the balance

12/15/86—Garcia's first show after his recovery at the Oakland Coliseum

7/87—*In the Dark* is released and shoots up the charts

1/89—*Dylan and the Dead* is released

10/89—*Built to Last* is released

7/26/90—Brent Mydland dies of a drug overdose in his home in Lafayette, California

9/90—*Without a Net* is released

9/7/90—Vince Welnick plays his first show with the Grateful Dead

9/15/90—Bruce Hornsby begins filling in on keyboards

4/15/91—*One From the Vault* is released, featuring a show from 8/13/75 at the Great American Music Hall in San Francisco

10/25/91—Bill Graham dies in a helicopter crash while returning from a Huey Lewis concert at the Concord Pavillion in Concord, California

11/91—*Infrared Roses* is released.

5/92—*Two from the Vault* is released, containing recordings from the Shrine Auditorium in Los Angeles from 8/23/68 and 8/24/68

11/93—Dick's Picks, Volume 1 is released, containing a show from 12/19/73 in Tampa, Florida

1/19/94—The Grateful Dead are inducted into the Rock and Roll Hall of Fame; since Garcia can't make it, the other band members take along a cardboard cutout of the guitarist

3/94—Dan Healy leaves the Grateful Dead

6/25/95—Three fans are struck by lightning at a show in Washington, D.C.

7/2/95—3,000 fans riot at a show in Indiana; the band criticizes their behavior in a scathing message via the Internet

7/9/95—Jerry Garcia plays his last show at Soldier Field in Chicago

8/9/95—Jerry Garcia dies of heart failure at a drug rehab center in Forest Knolls, California; communication on the Internet reaches such proportions that many addresses are forced to shut down

8/12/95—Fans gather at the Polo Fields in Golden Gate Park for a mass wake; surviving band and family members share their memories of Garcia

12/8/95—The band announces they will no longer be touring as the Grateful Dead.

"Built to Last"

Discography

Grateful Dead (Warner Brothers, 1967)

Anthem of the Sun (Warner Brothers, 1968)

Aoxomoxoa (Warner Brothers, 1969)

Live/Dead (Warner Brothers, 1969)

Workingman's Dead (Warner Brothers, 1970)

American Beauty (Warner Brothers, 1970)

Grateful Dead Live, aka *Skull & Roses, Skullfuck* (Warner Brothers, 1971)

Europe '72 (Warner Brothers, 1972)

History of the Grateful Dead, Volume 1—Bear's Choice (Warner Brothers, 1973)

Wake of the Flood (Grateful Dead Records, 1973)

From the Mars Hotel (Grateful Dead Records, 1974)

Skeletons from the Closet (Warner Brothers, 1974)

Blues for Allah (Grateful Dead Records, 1975)

Steal Your Face (Grateful Dead Records, 1976)

Terrapin Station (Arista, 1977)

What a Long Strange Trip It's Been (Warner Brothers, 1977)

Shakedown Street (Arista, 1978)

Go to Heaven (Arista, 1980)

Reckoning (Arista, 1981)

Dead Set (Arista, 1981)

In the Dark (Arista, 1987)

Dylan and the Dead (Arista, 1989)

Built to Last (Arista, 1989)

Without a Net (Arista, 1990)

One from the Vault (Arista, 1991)

Infrared Roses (Arista, 1991)

Two from the Vault (Arista, 1992)

Dick's Picks, Volume 1 (Arista, 1993)

Solo Efforts by Jerry Garcia

Hooteroll (Rykodisc, 1971)

Garcia (Grateful Dead Records, 1972)

Heavy Turbulence (With Merle Saunders, 1972)

Live at Keystone (With Merle Saunders, 1974)

Compliments (Grateful Dead Records, 1974)

Reflections (Grateful Dead Records, 1976)

Cats under the Stars (Arista, 1978)

Run for the Roses (Arista, 1982)

Almost Acoustic (Grateful Dead Records, 1988)

Jerry Garcia Band (Arista, 1991)

Garcia/Grisman (Acoustic Disc, 1991)

Not for Kids Only (with David Grisman,
Acoustic Disc, 1993)

Solo Efforts by Mickey Hart

Rolling Thunder (Grateful Dead Records, 1972)

Diga (Rykodisc, 1976)

The Apocolypse Now Sessions (Rykodisc, 1989)

Dafos (Rykodisc, 1989)

Music to Be Born by (Rykodisc, 1989)

Planet Drum (Rykodisc, 1991)

Solo Efforts by Bob Weir

Ace (Grateful Dead Records, 1972)

Kingfish (Grateful Dead Records, 1976)

Heaven Help the Fool (Arista, 1978)

Bobby and the Midnites (Arista, 1981)

King Biscuit Flower Hour Presents Kingfish (King Biscuit Flower Hour, 1995)

"Leader of the Band"

A Trivia Tribute to Jerry Garcia

Everyone knows Jerry Garcia was missing his middle right finger, just as everyone knows someone who has one of his mildly psychedelic ties. But did you know . . .

. . . that when he was five, he saw his father, José, drown?

. . . that he failed the eighth grade for refusing to do homework and eventually dropped out of high school?

. . . that he joined the Army to get away from San Francisco, but ended up stationed at the Presidio?

. . . that he received two court-martials and eight AWOLs during his nine-month stint in the service?

. . . that he and Robert Hunter appeared together in the early 1960s as "Bob and Jerry," playing bluegrass?

. . . that a young Bill Kreutzmann sold him a banjo at Dana Morgan's Music Store?

. . . that Garcia himself sometimes gave banjo and guitar lessons at the store?

. . . that in 1971 he had a Gibson guitar stolen from backstage at the Hollywood Palladium?

. . . that he was credited as "musical and spiritual adviser" on the Jefferson Airplane album *Surrealistic Pillow?*

. . . that in the 1970s he created music and sound effects for *Invasion of the Body Snatchers* and a few Roger Corman films?

. . . that in January 1985 when he was arrested in Golden Gate Park for freebasing cocaine in his BMW, the reason police approached the car was because the registration was expired?

. . . that after a diabetic coma in 1986, he had to relearn the guitar with the help of friends?

. . . that a frogfish Garcia befriended while scuba diving in Kona, Hawaii, is named Little Jerry?

. . . that he wore a tuxedo without a tie to his Valentine's Day, 1994, wedding to Deborah Koons?

. . . that before his death, Garcia's original paintings sometimes fetched up to $20,000?

. . . that close to 25,000 fans gathered to say good-bye to Garcia on Aug. 13, 1995?

. . . that on the October 31, 1995, episode of *Roseanne,* the title character named her baby "Jerry Garcia Conner" and dedicated the episode to the memory of Jerry Garcia?